Cracks in the Universe

CHARLES TOMLINSON was born in Stoke on Trent in 1927. He studied at Cambridge with Donald Davie and taught at the University of Bristol from 1957 until his retirement. He has published many collections of poetry as well as volumes of criticism and translation, and has edited the *Oxford Book of Verse in English Translation* (1980). His poetry has won international recognition and has received many prizes in Europe and the United States, including the 1993 Bennett Award from the *Hudson Review*; the New Criterion Poetry Prize, 2002; the Premio Internazionale di Poesia Ennio Flaiano, 2001; and the Premio Internazionale di Poesia Attilio Bertolucci, 2004. He is an Honorary Fellow of the American Academy of the Arts and Sciences and of the Modern Language Association. Charles Tomlinson was made a CBE for his contribution to literature in 2001.

T0163078

Also by Charles Tomlinson from Carcanet

Poetry
Annunciation
Door in the Wall
Selected Poems
The Vineyard Above the Sea
Skywriting

Prose
American Essays
Metamorphoses: Poetry and Translation

CHARLES TOMLINSON

Cracks in the Universe

OxfordPoets

CARCANET

First published in Great Britain in 2006 by
Carcanet Press Limited
Alliance House
Cross Street
Manchester M2 7AQ

A CIP catalogue record for this book is available from the British Library
ISBN 1 903039 79 7
978 1 903039 79 3

The publisher acknowledges financial assistance from Arts Council England

Typeset by XL Publishing Services, Tiverton
Printed and bound in England by SRP Ltd, Exeter

to Brenda

Acknowledgements

Acknowledgements are due to the editors of the following: *Agenda*, *Angelaki*, the *Bristol and Gloucestershire Archaeological Society Newsletter*, the *Critical Quarterly*, *Cultural* (Madrid), *Letras Libres*, *Metre*, the *New Criterion*, *OxfordPoets 2001*, the *Paris Review*, *Poetry Ireland Review*, *PN Review*, *Resine*, *The Review*, *Southwest Review*, the *Times Literary Supplement* and the *Yale Review*; and to Faber and Faber, the Globe and the Wordsworth Trust, Penguin Books, Shoestring Press, Stride and Birmingham Health Authority. The following poems appeared in the *Hudson Review*: 'Apples', 'Above the City', 'A View from the Shore', 'The Upstate Freeze' and 'Vessel'.

Contents

Above the City

It would be good
to pass the afternoon
under this lucid sky,
strolling at rooftop level
this city above the city,
all the tubular protruberances,
chimneys, triangular skylights,
sheds that have lost their gardens
spread before one. The details
are not delicate up here
among the pipes and stacks,
the solid immovables, and yet
each outcrop affords
a fresh vista
to the *promeneur solitaire* –
though only the pigeons
are properly equipped
to go on undeterred
by changes of level where
one of their flat-footed
number suddenly launches itself
off the cornice sideways
taking its shadow with it
and bursts into dowdy flower,
blossoms in feathery mid-air to become
all that we shall never be,
condemned to sit
watching from windows
the life of those airy acres
we shall never inherit.

New York

A View from the Shore

I woke this morning
to find Brooklyn Bridge
festooned with a fringe of vineleaves
along the entire length
of the frame of its steel harp
and beyond: an aquatic ivy
was clasping the stone piers and climbing
towards the topmost cables:
drivers could no doubt see
the flicker of leaves
ascending past them and – glancing down –
even sun picking out the spear tips
where shoreside reeds pressed on the eye
their foreground to a car-crammed vista: here
overnight a crisis in the environment
had found its vent
and out of the hemmed-in cornucopia
that was nature once, had started
unstoppably to pour itself back
through this crack in the universe
on this outflanked riverbank
where the triumph of suspended steel
and its aftermath
had first begun.

New Jersey – New York

The mergings of cars, the chains of light
Announcing bridges, intersections,
They would see it all differently
From apartment windows,
Not nervously alert to the swervings
As traffic swings out to fill the thoroughfare
That is feeding one in – between
Lights and lights, buildings and buildings –
With a million cars, each one
A travelling eye
Letting things occur, letting them appear
As they will, the city itself another nature
Cutting into the density of spaces
With its stepped-back panoramas, the place
As merciless and beautiful as the universe.

A Name on the Map

for Judith Saunders

I ask myself what Fishkill must be like.
There is a river pouring into town
Under its elegant bridge; I scan the house-fronts
For their carpentered rhythmic trim, baroque
Curlicues in a wilderness that was.
It is the name drives the imagination back
To when the fish were plentiful, the Indians
With wet, red arms spearing up shad on shad
Out of the falls. Next time I cross the state,
I shall investigate the curio shops,
And perhaps recover from the dust
Some modest sketch, composed – though left unsigned
By the hand of (could it be?) Church or Bierstadt –
One closing winter afternoon just when
The artist was not thinking about mountains:
'Fishkill in February', in whites and gold,
And let into the sky in bold relief,
The cross above the college towards sunset.

The Upstate Freeze

for Fred Busch

That spring the sap had risen when
The ice took hold. Under a sky
That was grey-black it lay
In packed particles that were the same colour.
Risen sap froze in trunks and branches
And tree limbs began to crack from within,
Whole trunks ripped open white
Though not with snow or ice: bare
Tree interiors unhusked themselves there
Smelling of secret places, an intoxication
Of sap filling each nostril. The tree
On which blue herons yearly nested
Lay tipped aside, a sanctuary smashed.
The world was lead and it had blown apart.

Apples

Across the orchards of abandoned farms,
Walking the hills above the town,
We found that fallen apples kept their flavour.
It had grown more various and precise,
A measure of varieties no longer sold.
What we lack is an archaeology of apples,
But apple is neither coin nor arrowhead.
Going back down our feet encountered
Among the grass the graves of apple growers
Buried beside their crop, hidden obstructions
Slowing our descent. I do not think
That Eve discovered evil in an apple,
As its sweeter knowledge filled her mouth.
Today, with Adirondack winter on us,
We watch the fire and scent the apple-wood,
Counting the trails we can no longer follow,
The hills around us one long sierra of snow.

Four for David Smith

to Paula

1 Interior for Exterior

They tried to bring the whole of the view
into the room. But the strain
of space four walls could not contain
forced them at last to see
you could let in the outlines only
of hill, house, tree
to compose a cosmos circling,
signs in supple flight that show
which way the winds blow,
angels about to alight on a pinpoint
but who keep on flowing.

2 The Timeless Clock

The circular ride was shaking it to pieces,
the same track, the same worn ratchets
slewed out of kilter
but pacing shakily on,
falling apart as it strained towards
the open air,
the crumbling clouds reshaping,
the continuity of rivers —
all that a circle cannot hold.

3 Hudson River Landscape

Not the sublime.
There is a time for that also,
but the present occasion
is more a question
of how do you hold a conversation
and with whom. To make that clear
I have turned my house into a foundry:
Picasso, González, Miró
are all welcome here. Where are the trees?
These are the branches of the trees –
I have invited space in
to pick them clean. I have written them
on the air
like a letter that will arrive
by first post and the fable
of the first day turn fact,
the light equable.

4 Bolton Landing

The ballet
of steel
beneath
a winter sky:
it was a man
made these
bare boughs.

David Smith, American sculptor (1906–65). He placed many of his works, their metallic surfaces reflecting the colours of nature, in the open air at Bolton Landing.

Recalling Orson Welles

When you brought the ceiling
into the picture –
prison and precision –
what it revealed
was that the space
silently clothing us
was not infinite
but contained
both the place and persons
in the case:
under the vague
ceiling of the years
you went on talking
with all the brio
of the twenty-five-year-old
and the tales you told
on the screen
lost their conviction
and the meaning
you had gathered once
into those interiors
sealed and solidified
by the fifth wall
overhead which said:
here you are what you are.

Providence

Morning shadows waiting to surprise us
Across the white façades under the jut of eaves,
Houses are accurate sundials in such light –
Though it is less the time on them one reads
Than intimations of the day's advance
From satin on the sun-greyed cedar fence
To porch and gable, roof-pitch, balcony,
All the invitations of geometry
To measure time by the rule of spaces
From the dawn coldness to the evening cool,
Sunpath of providential emphases.

Rhode Island

Thomas Jones in Naples, 1782

He preferred the unglazed windows of the houses,
The door left open onto dark inside,
That made the radiant stucco of the wall
Seem like a daily bread the eye might feed on.
A day like this, how little one has need of
To make that little much: the nondescript
Ochre paint that brings what light there is
Marked out by shade across a shut door's panels,
The stepped-up levels of the town beyond
Dustily receding, plane by plane,
Towards the background domes and spires – glories
Unaccounted where the skyline celebrates
The white shirt of a workman on the roof.

Stellar Friendship

after Nietzsche

We were friends: we have become
strangers to each other.
We were two ships
each with its course and aim –
ships that lay
in the same harbour,
under the one sun and on a day
they seemed to have reached their goal.
But then the force
of what it was we had to do
drove us apart and into
strange seas and zones
that must change our faces.
Even now, our paths
might intersect and we
celebrate that encounter
as before. But to become
strangers is the law
that governs us both,
and just by that
we shall measure
our meaning for each other,
where there is an immense
invisible track, an orbit
pinning the dark,
in which our ways
and ends, bending
beyond our lost beginnings,
can reconcile in a cosmic curve
friendship as separate as the stars.

The Pupil

Who painted these pictures that take in
   The whole curvature of the visual hemisphere,
Where the gables and the roofs appear
   As if they were the minims and the blocks
Of an entire universe that freezes, flows
   And then recomposes itself beneath
A different light? The humble and colossal
   Pissarro – the adjectives are Cézanne's,
Who painted side by side with this man
   Of humbler gifts, 'to learn from him'.

La Rochelle

The whiteness of the city and its towers
Recalls the trade in salt that made it rich.
Now time has soiled the limestone of façades,
And yet this light of spring can still retrieve
Their saline sharpness, as another evening
Ferries out the sun beyond a harbour
Bristling with the masts of anchored yachts:
Beneath their hulls the ballet of reflections
Ripples and twists in rhythm with the swell,
The jostled whiteness of disjointed spars
Gone gold already in the alchemic sun.

Monet's Giverny

A certain fierceness in the sky, a blaze
Cuts out the verticals of the poplar trees
Against its steepness, so that only they
(The wind is rising through their ruffled leaves)
Serve to record the bright pitch of a day
Whose brightness asks no more than this – to burn
To the answering scrutiny of an eye
Fed by the fresh resilience of trees,
A palisade against the climbing clouds
And all that is tugging out of shape
This pact with time, this urgent landscape.

Les Joueurs de Football

In the Douanier's picture
Les Joueurs de Football,
even I who
ever since the day
I was forced out onto
a cricket pitch
have detested all
forms of team sport,
can see that the ball
in this charming ballet
is a rugby ball, and that
the four players, two
to a side (each
provided with an identical
moustache) are Art's reply
to the banalities of Life.
Perhaps the smallness of the pitch
mirrors the ever smaller studio
Rousseau must move into
each time he tried to retrench,
to find money for his paints
or for his *soirées familiales et artistiques*
at which he played his violin
and even sang. The wall
of remarkably small autumnal trees
that surrounds this scene
on three sides lies
open to a turquoise sky
across which clouds (one
like the snout of a beneficent
saurian) declare
a change in the air and season,
hinting at all that may yet occur
undreamt by any footballer –
even those who struggle
for possession of an egg-like
ball – as nature brews
overhead its unending future,

its heterogeneity we do not understand
of a field without obvious rules,
goal posts or goals.

Henri Rousseau, known as the Douanier, French painter, 1844–1910.

Bread and Stone

The fragment of a loaf, rejected, stale:
As beautiful as any stone, it bears
Seams, scars, a dust of flour and like a stone
If it could unfold its history,
Would speak of its time in darkness and of light
Drawing it towards the thing it is,
Hard to the hand, an obstacle to sight,
Out of an untold matrix. If a son
Ask bread of you, would stone be your reply?
Let the differentiating eye
Rest on this, and for the moment read
The seed of nourishment in it as the sun
Reveals this broken bread as textured stone,
Served out as a double feast for us
On the cloth of the commonplace miraculous.

Fantasia in Limestone

'A fox head', you say and I
'A limestone spatula,
ready for use, but what use?'
You might well think
stone could repel all metaphor,
a mere flake of bone
from the skeleton of this hill,
but there, too, in the act
of saying, metaphor looms:
no fact stands free
from its own reflection and we
with the proverbial milk
imbibe it, a glad ghost
dancing airily under the eye of reason:
this second creation,
as intricately unforeseen
as the first, and both
untwining in relation,
glance towards each other where they spin
on the needle-point of mind,
twin births, children of chance.

Choice

If I must choose
between stone and cloud
let me not refuse
either, imagining
that one or the other must be
foremost in hierarchy
of thing over thing:
nothing is king
in this weather-swept world –
years shaping stone,
cloud crowds amassed
in a single noon,
and each sight so various
whatever meets the eye
seems to stare back at us
in sharp mutuality.
I turn away
from the rising cloudscapes
and what do I see
at my feet but a pebble
as pocked and rounded as they,
like a minuscule cloud-copy,
but here for millennia
or as long as human hand
takes up such tokens of time
from the generous ground.

Pebble

Take it up between thumb and index:
A stone conundrum you might call
This pebble of limestone. Fragments
Of identities struggle here to be themselves,
Searching for certainty but preyed upon
By a dozen images. A circle
At the pebble's centre makes a roving pupil
That is content to blur and be merely
A vague stomachless navel, then
An unmistakable mouth wide open
To sing a silent top note,
Yet transforms itself even as you wait to hear that note
Into half a head with two eyes
And then decides to be only a snout
With nostrils. A single ear
Begins to sprout from the irresolute stone
And next ventures to appear
As proud, wind-tossed locks of hair
Distinct above the flock of petrine pretenders
Whose entire mass now marches towards,
Threatens to carry me away from what I am
And into their pebble desert of unending babble.
I must fling it far off towards anonymity
This multitudinous changeling and let it stay
With its fellows forever on their prosaic pathway.

Chinchón

Trees in this landscape
signal the presence of a river.
A side-road leads us on –
parched grass, a rock horizon –
and winds us towards
a town watched over by
the blind eyes of a ruined castle:
this is Chinchón.
December a week away,
the place is half deserted.
The square that can be converted
into a bullring or a theatre
awaits the arrival of actors
to perform the piece by Lope de Vega
promised on the playbills.
We sit in the bar of the parador
in the midst of a floral display
on blue tiles, over a drink
that creates a circle of warmth
in the growing chill
and is also called Chinchón.
Aniseed. Anise is
what these dry fields feed,
with its yellowish-white small flowers
and liquorish-flavoured seed:
we are drinking the distillation
of Spain – a certain pungency
which is not unsweet, like the heat
and tang in the Spanish aspirate.
The sky looks down on our departure
through each one of the blind eyes
of the castle. The car
is a lost beetle in the vast
spreading amplitude of Castile
expanding around us. Snowflakes
over the far Guadarrama
feel for the mountain spine
that reaches to the heights like a line
of surf suddenly breaking on the peaks. Below,
burning stubble in the fields

is turning the twilight blue
and losing the thread of the road we are on,
Chinchón lamplit behind us, Chinchón gone.

November in Aranjuez

for Ricardo Jesús Sola Buil

Trunks stand ankle–deep in leaves.
    Immense, each leaf has the proportions
Of a discarded broken fan. The court
    Came here in summer to escape the heat,
Did not stay long enough perhaps
    To greet the fallen foliage, their ears
Alert to the underfoot snap and splash,
    The crackle of autumn. The park is haunted
By the ghosts of their intentions. Colonnades,
    Paths, perspectives, squares, the palace
Is the place, its fountains still play on,
    And the season cannot cease flattering the statues
Radiant in the astonishment of an autumn sun.

Santiago de Compostela

Granite is the stone
in church and fishmarket –
except for the marble
where fish lie glittering:
the strong woman
who rules this place
wrestles a live conger
out of its tub:
we watch it snake
slippery in her grip –
she lets it writhe until
we have looked our fill,
then aims it back
waterwards and next draws out
(trawling a lower depth
on the scale of being)
a lamprey, all circular mouth
and inevitable eye:
it challenges her grasp,
seeing and seizing
a dead fish from her slab
in a single swoop
with that primordial sucker,
accurate as Iago
killer of Moors,
ancient as granite.

was led by a woman –
a hand on each horn:
she, stepping backwards,
encouraged its advance,
her man between plough shafts
setting the course
where the rye had failed
and maize must grow now:
they stopped to talk
to us strangers at the granite wall and
with a loquacious pride
told over their possessions –
two tractors, a car, the land:
the beast stood there
like an interested listener,
patiently translating
inside its ox's brain
what was being said –
rather like me, as I
tried to penetrate their sibilant Portuguese:
it loomed in a silhouette
that resembled the statue of an ox,
but not for long, and when
it must move on once again
took up the tenor of its advance
in contrary motion, a slow
music, step by step
fading across that field
whose half-light hid
a terrain of scattered stones
autumn would submerge in grain.

Lessons

1 On a Picture of Burslem by Leonard Brammer

He was that quiet man who taught us art –
Or rather left us to ourselves to learn.
I copied mannequins from Chirico
Hoping for recognition. Was it despair
Drove him to ignore his herd of boys?
'The self-taught man' – and that was us –
'Is taught by a very ignorant person.'
Constable said that. I saw it then,
As he issued sheets of paper, kept his peace.
There was no secret he would teach me
Although he knew them. Look at this thirties view.
It took me years to see that Stoke-on-Trent
Offered a theme for words. The waste, flat ground
Stretches behind roofs and bottle ovens,
And seems a lake beneath such pallid light,
All are on foot, the car not yet arrived.
He was a Lowry, not a Chirico man.
I'd traced the outlines and that didn't please him –
If only he had shown me how to draw.
This forgery of silhouettes was all he saw
And warned the class against, much to my shame,
Though being a decent, gentle sort of man
Blamed only 'someone', never spoke my name.

2 The Fruits of Ignominy

'An ignominious failure, Tomlinson.'
An ignominious teacher was my thought.
I bit it back and lowering my head
Accepted the rebuke, as I'd been taught.
If they could teach me that, why couldn't he
Teach me arithmetic? What he had said
He aimed from the doorway coming in,
An actor with a nervous audience:
Brandishing the sheets of their exam,
He trod the boards and taught me what I am:
Words were the sole abstractions I could use –

Words like *ignominious*, words and shapes
And what I could not grasp I might transfuse
Into lines and colours. I can now reclaim
Neither his cast of features nor his name.

3 The Bicycle

'You'll never ride a bike,' my father said.
He was the instructor – and at swimming too:
I never mastered that. A boy I knew
Took my cycling seriously in hand
And if my breast-stroke had been left to him
I have no doubt I would have learned to swim.
It was the bike that opened up those spaces
Beyond the smoking confines of the town,
Found me what swimming never would have shown –
George Eliot's Staffordshire and Wordsworth's north,
Though north was north of Leek, the Roaches there
(The rocks it meant), Rudyard was Windermere:
And if you could not make it to the spot,
You could relocate the place it was not:
I moved the Brontë parsonage further south
And Heathcliff roamed the moorlands far from Haworth.
Praise to the bicycle, transport of the muse:
It brought the only news that always stayed news.

4 In Memory of Agnes Beverley Burton

I did not learn to draw until that lady
(Not easy to please) saw my incompetence
At sketching trees and, 'Simplify,' she said,
'Follow only the leading lines of things,'
And commandeered my hand to imitate
A cluster of boughs, then sped it on
To face another jutting ganglion
Where both eye and trunk were made to feel
The presence of a directed force, taught me to see
The heaves of structure up the entire tree
And plot its course from roots to summit
In whatever season, where the branches
Hung simplified by winter, simplified by leaves.

5 To Nora Christabel Pennet

Benign aunt, sister to the above –
The idiom of epitaphs cannot catch
Her gentleness or her gentility:
She did not force my hand, but led me through
Landscapes of Ancient China, bound in silk:
A new space opened under a new light,
Though 'Pine Scent in the Clarity of Snow'
Taught me, not how to draw, but how to write.
Spent twenty years out East and then kept shop
In the provinces, painted when she could
Those curling roofs round courtyards and the fens
Of Lincolnshire. In *Modern German Art*,
A gift outright – her last – and not a loan,
Ernst's 'Bride of the Wind' distracted me
Back to the brush, the vagaries of chance:
She had hinted a new poise, a way to dance.

6 The Boy on the Sick-Bed

The boy on the sick-bed, now the man who writes,
Gazes – he lacks the strength to stare –
Out of the window through the rain-soaked air
Tinged by the smoke and by a fringe of fire
Where the steel-mills were and are no longer.
He asks his mother to draw what she can see,
She picks up the pencil he has thrown aside,
Narrows her eyes in taking steady hold
And draws the serried chimneys on the roofs,
Each with its jagged terracotta crown –
All the regality he will ever own
And lose before he finds the place again
And letting fall the pencil, takes up the pen.

The Photograph

in memoriam Edwin Albert Raybould

All these men are dead. One of them I knew.
From the silhouette of a blackened pithead
They eye the camera we cannot see –
Collar-and-tie men from the offices –
Brylcreemed hair, bunches of hands on laps –,
Miners in mufflers and with caps as flat
And comfortable as their Midland 'a's.
The one I knew? Sixth from the left and standing.
His history: Passchendaele, Ypres, the Mons Star,
The wounds he kept concealed to get the job
In a hard time – now fireman down this pit,
The one who lights the fuses and breaks through
Into untouched seams waiting for the pick.
Slagheaps, already greening-over, rise
Like a range of hills, faint figures there
Bend down to glean the fragments of those coals
Which, blown into a glimmer, then a glow,
Will feed their fires. It was the camera
And not the man behind it sought them out,
As unregarded as the shrapnel wounds
The fireman hid. He smiles and keeps his peace,
His good leg braced to move once poses cease.

Little Eve and the Miners

Little Eve looks through the slatted gate
To watch from her garden the miners pass.
They, leaning over and peering down in,
Offer her apples from their snappin' tin.

Returning apple-less at the end of shift,
In blackface and with startling eyes, they pass
The garden, abandoned by little Eve now,
To bath on their hearth before the coals' heaped glow.

In '35

There was that pub at Cobridge
whose landlord, a blackshirt though a pleasant man,
followed the local usage
and allowed the children of his customers
to wait for them in the kitchen.
I remember the cheese on the table there.
I didn't touch it because of the mites
whose activity fascinated and repelled me.
Not once did I see the landlord in his uniform –
perhaps he owned none. Moseley
visited the place – the place not the pub –
but was never elected here. The populace
were soberer than that leader urging them
to put on their blackshirts, and to march in step
instead of downing their drinks at the bar,
their children warm before the backroom fire.

I Was a Child

when I played Tasmania
in the Empire Day pageant:
that was May twenty-fourth – Victoria's
birthday, another age in fact
and the old queen's head
still reigned on half the currency:
as I climbed up to the stage
robed and shoeless,
a splinter from the floor
penetrated my naked foot as keen
as a Tasmanian arrow.

Aubade

Those dawn flutes from *Daphnis and Chloë*
    Made me get up to see one day
Whether the dawn was like that and the way
    Hills above the city looked as smoke
Came drifting up through half-light,
    Meeting red embers from the lower sky:
Out there, far from Illyria,
    Cold dew, condensing on the grass,
Soon found me out, and sodden knees
    Woke me, a trousered boy, to where I was,
Above the steel works and the dawning line
    Of the canal by Wedgwood's factory,
The spot the boy in him had called Etruria.

Seasons

With the change of light
New forms of shade invade the house:
The window-frame, cut out in black,
    Lies beside the sun on surfaces
Not seen before – the walls that we had come
    To take for granted, as the unchanging shape
Of home. Why does this repetition
    Return out of the sky each year
As manna falling, dew upon the sense,
    Renewal of the place one finds it in?
The year is repeating itself afresh:
    It seems that we are nearing now
The roadstead of Cytherea, and hear
    The music of our sailing and arrival
In a major key. We shall not harbour there,
    But take only time enough to breathe
The perfume of the lime-trees flowering where
    They meet the ocean odour in a mingled scent
Of home-coming and departure. What is that shade
    Spreading through the water – stain or shoal?
We feel the waves repeating themselves beneath us,
    Like the palpitation of light within that window
We left behind, before the spring went down
    Under oceanic summer, into tidal year.

In the Valley

Walking west, I could no longer find
    The spot the sun set only yesterday.
A cloud already shut the valley in,
    But darker than the cloud, its shadow
Spread across the valley floor
    In leisurely inundation. You could sense
Above the moving mass the solar force
    By the dark that went on rising
Round the sombre columns of the trunks
    Between sward and sky. My eye
Combed the shoreline of this flood
    But the shore fell sheer towards
The endlessly advancing tide. The trees,
    Already dense with summer, rooted
In that country of the blind, rose to where
    A light withheld that knew and yet
Would not reveal the secret of their green.
    Lethe rose beneath the layered leaves:
I thought of the murk of Dis, of lavaflow,
    But this was one of mercy's moments:
Lightly I trod between the shadowed earth
    And the unseen horizon, entering
A cool as of water. The drift
    Of a universe, rehearsing its own end,
Stood at a pause, in a present
    Brimmed with unexhausted time
Between the hidden sun and the awaiting dark.

Tree Talk

occurs when two
tortuous branches grind
one against the other and emit
as they rock in air
not cradling coos
but a lament of all you lose
in life's constrictions
like a wounded violin
a slow and comfortless
adagio scaling
higher and higher in a thin
scream of ultimate
rejection, of final
disaffection at
all that conspires
to plant thorn on thorn
in the yielding flesh
of innocence betrayed:
it goes on
penetrating bonewards
(where is the greensward now?)
in a way that only music can
as it quits all keys
and gasping in atonality
refuses to return
to the home note
or float dreamwards
on the drowsing stream of
a fawn's afternoon:
Venus is not here:
only the divine
marquis offering you the whip
as a hand-up on
the intersection of two
untuned almost twigs
that even in their twiggery know
that as the wind goes down they
must shut up.

Dragonflies

Dragonflies
flock to this garden
like swallows in autumn
(it is high summer):
such glamour
in predation, scissor-jawed
and single-minded,
they radar their way
past obstacles,
flying in formation,
pilots who are their own craft,
speed their sole stratagem:
cold that means death to them
makes them begin
to disappear just as the dark
comes cooling in.

Swifts

Swifts do not sing:
what they do well
is sleep on the wing
moving always higher and higher
in their almost entirely
aerial existence, alighting
only to nest, lay eggs,
rear their young and then
back to the airways
to teach them there
the art of high-speed darting
with narrow swept-back wings
and streamlined bodies:
when swifts descend
they cannot perch, they cling
by hook-shaped toes
to walls and so crawl
into sheltered cavities, into gaps
in eaves and church towers
where they can nest. Summer visitors
they seem always about to leave
and when they finally do
scream in their hundreds
that the time is now,
that the south awaits,
that he who procrastinates
has only the cold to explore
for those succulent insects
who are no longer there.

In Autumn

Moon rose, a clear
crescent. At dawn
a deer came down the slope
in fugitive distinctness
and the sun caught
the glimmer of gossamers
draping a wet bush. Where
is the hare bound
that parts the grasses? –
he is caution's creature
unlike the pheasant horde,
birds so tame
they must be kicked
off the ground into the air
to ignite the stone-
cold heart of the hunter
beside the artificial lake where
the passing moon
is pausing to inspect itself.

In January

After dark weeks of rain, the world
   Seems shut round on itself, itselves:
There is a secrecy, a veiling back that you
   Will never penetrate although you hear
A hundred voices tell it, far and near –
   Rain on the roof, wind in the leafless tree –
Or catch the sound that two streams make
   In moving across the territory
They divide between them before meeting.
   The slant rain, the receding light,
The closing-in of fields gone grey
   Beneath shadowless trees, refuse the blame
We would attach to them by robbing with a name
   The completeness of the nameless presence here:
'Miserable' – we try to make it fit,
   But weather washes our lament away
With a susurration that does not even scorn
   Our refusal of the encounter: our grain
Of misery waiting to sprout and spread
   Is not of the kin of twilight or the steady rain.

The Rain Is Over

The rain is over, the sky
has fallen in bright blue pieces:
you can no more pick them up
than before they fell
becoming sky-shards,
segments, a sliver
bisecting the road
with its shining chasm
which you straddle,
look into and see the way
the crowns of tree after leafless tree
have come down with it
crowding this narrow sky-pond
like underwater vegetation:
threads of what went on overhead
catch at the eye
wherever you gaze on ground,
each seam of light,
each bright stitch
a reminder of that perfection
before the heavens fell
which now − night coming on −
lie holding the stars.

Jaws

of cloud dispute
the sky of late afternoon,
the going sun suspended
before it drops behind the horizon
and leaves darkness to debate
whether these predatory shapes
are there still hanging in the black air
as the cold bright stars of Sagittarius
climb glittering and disclose
the prospect of their voyages, an invitation
to a freshly minted moon
to edge its way
towards the galaxy
until it stands mid-sky to show
the place where that unmappable murk
hung below and now not one
of those drifting saurians remains
beneath the high clear chart
stretched between earth and zenith.

Across the Dark

With so much sound below the silence, we
    Are left to make out what we cannot see –
That sonorous cavity between hollowed banks
    Where the current comes rushing through,
Advancing melodiously beneath the cry
    Of vigilant owls. They answer one another,
Deepening distance with their calls
    And – menace and music in a single note –
Fence round their little empires with the sound.
    Under it all, the tones of water tell
The distances that it has travelled through
    Where water, tonguing its song from stones,
Asks speech of us to measure and re-murmur
    Those fluid shapes that now besiege the ear
Sluicing past us, chiselling a way,
    To arrive, through limestone, time, palpable here.

Westminster Bridge from the Eye

written to be read in the Globe Theatre

What is a sonnet? 'Take these fourteen lines
Of *Paradise Lost*,' Wordsworth told a friend –
(A gathering music with no rhymes to end
Each line) 'The image of a sphere or dewdrop,
An orbicular body,' he went on.
This sonnet – globe within The Globe – is one
Way to double the sonnet circle. Take
The Eye also. From its orbicular cabins
You see Westminster Bridge extend as he
Never saw it – the same bridge with its view
Where ships, towers, domes, theatres lie below,
And now that clambering disparity –
Corbusier's children quarrelling for the sky –
In a paradise lost that Wordsworth did not know.

In the Wind

This animal hold,
bodily pull
against gravitation,
against the vertical, this
obstruction I lean into and swim,
this same force overhead
is unlayering with ease,
peeling apart
dark continents of cloud,
getting down to sun,
then letting it filter and flood
the sky I am wading towards,
out of which its vast breath
is prying apart the ties
in this middle place
of tiles, trees, chimneys
between the abyss above us
and the abyss below, the snapped boughs
barring my way as I crackle through.

Returning

My long-legged shadow
pointing east
measures out the sundown
across half a field:
I have become
a phantom giant and my home
as I approach it
seems unsure of me
and shrinks
as if to contain its threatened fire.
I turn
in the direction of the going sun —
it has suddenly gone
and the whole scene
grown dark and vast
in my wake, swallowing
the scale of my magnification
in a single quenching shade
that puts out all
including horizon
and my own tall shadow.
I turn again
to that glowing smallness
and I cross
the remainder of the field between us,
entering its jewel to become
my own right size
by the habitable light
inside the domestic diamond,
a Gulliver gratified.

In the Mirror

Angled towards the window,
the mirror sees things I cannot see –
even brings indoors to me
lost landscapes, vignettes
of cattle browsing beneath trees
that could have been painted.

'Why do you,' she asks,
'keep looking at yourself?'
I am not 'looking at myself' I explain
'I am looking at a train
that has just entered the picture
in the silent distance.'

I can see time
through the mirror
by the town clock, but in reverse,
as if a curse
had been put on it
to travel only towards yesterday.

And now the train has disappeared.
Where have the cattle gone?
Of all the herd
only one to be seen –
a black shape in soliloquy
on a deserted green.

Gazing here,
Narcissus would have failed
to examine his own image,
letting his grimace stare
out of a dead centre –
margins are where true happenings are.

A Rose from Fronteira

Head of a rose:
above the vase
a gaze widening –
hardly a face, and yet
the warmth has brought it forth
out of itself,
with all its folds, flakes, layers
gathered towards the world
beyond the window,
as bright as features,
as directed as a look:
rose, reader
of the book
of light.

Return to Valestrieri

What draws the mind
back to that place must be
things like the courtesy
of the man who, eyeing us strangers,
said: Have you seen our Roman bridge?
We saw it, crossed it, climbed
the far hillside to where
before a solitary house
a woman hovered
craving conversation and
launched into a lament –
her son – a mariner – had left her here,
he loved the place, but she
had no one to gratify
her need for daily talk. In the town itself
a forgetful population
had left for years the declaration
painted on a wall
in tall neat capitals:
It is an honour to serve fascism.

Mandarinas

Ten hours on a bus
(four more to go) and then
orange sellers climb aboard,
their high feminine voices
bringing refreshment with the cry
Mandarinas, mandarinas –
voices of such a pitch
as you never hear elsewhere
cutting through the air,
more instrument than blade,
reaching their top C
with utmost ease. Cortez
travelled that way possessed
by one last ambition – to be
Marquis of Oaxaca. Who
would not settle without rank or rancour
just to hear voices of orange sellers
as now we retrace his ground and theirs
in memory, miles and years away
in a land where no orange trees
flower from the temperate green and no
oranges grow to be gathered into sound?

November

The freeze sets in:
frost is returning
at three in the afternoon:
a seam of ore
opens at the valley head
under a single cloud. Kenner is dead –
the man who knew, saw, told
and clarified our seeing
privileged by his own:
requiescat in pace.

Morning

When we open the curtains,
will it be white or wet?
Will it (remembered) blaze back at us,
or shall we then forget

the grey irresolution
of rain against frost,
the distances melted away
and the far view lost

to a closed-in glance
across sweating flagstones,
catching what little light there is,
what wine-dark tones?

The choice is not ours to make,
so we await the chance
of weather's looming, loosening
in its long advance

up the valley reaches
and straight at our panes,
not to be predicted, contradicted:
let us draw back the curtains.

Frost

The sky is blank with a single vapour trail
    Warmed by a sunset we cannot see:
The coming freeze is hurrying it away,
    But listen: owls are shaping out the spaces
With their map of sounds. Sparks of stars
    Pierce through where darkness deepens,
Sharp with an undiluted light. Tomorrow we shall wake
    At the crackle of first footsteps grinding white.

On Snow

Low light is raking the entire field
   This winter afternoon. Sundown soon
Will alter the tone of snow from violet
   Where the shadow crosses it, to a smoky blue:
As they lengthen out, running together,
   So feather-fine those shadows seem:
The snow-light, trapped beneath them,
   Turns their texture to a smouldering glow
That threatens flame which a thickened gloom
   Slowly extinguishes. Overhead, a moonbow
Shares sky with Venus, while below
   The eyes through half-dark can decipher –
Cut into the surface in keen line –
   The pheasant's foot as a perfect arrow.

Resemblances

Woodland creaks like the cordage of a ship,
Spar over spar, rigged with fraying ropes –
The stems of creepers tautening, as boughs
Dip and release themselves from the wind's grip.
Intersecting, grinding on one another,
They groan above us as they bring to birth
Yet more resemblances. But let them be.
Enough that those battle sounds arrive
Inland with the smell of sea that is the real sea.

In a Glass of Water

Cheap jewels flash
up from the inside of a glass
which I am draining –
the glints and splinters
of a room, the green
exit sign and the red
bandanna round a woman's head –
such a horde of pinpoints
the eye is left confused
by pulsating water that transmits
the hand's hesitations as
liquid disappearing towards one
leaves a glass that is drained.

Vessel

I place water
in a glass pitcher
on the evening table
at the centre of the meal:
the stream outside
flashes back
late afternoon light:
water within the pitcher
rocks a little, prisoner
of glass and restive perhaps
to be what it once was
in full flow and not
this filled roundness,
now shaped and stilled.
But summon no Ondine
to embellish the thought,
pour out and drink
the caught coolness
that breathes here. Beyond the window,
in the high perfection
of a February night sky,
a winter moon has risen,
summoner of waters, filler of pitchers.
Below its slim sickle
travel the tones of the stream
that fed this still vessel
reflecting wine, fruit and bread.

The Holy Man

In at the gate
  A tramp comes sidling up:
'I called before,' – it's now eight –
  'But you were still sleeping.' He smiles
Like an actor who is perfectly sure
  His audience will approve of him, offers
To tell us his story in exchange
  For provision (the word is his) and lists
Tea, milk, candles and ointment:
  'I have been bitten by mosquitoes –
I bless them. They give only a love bite.
  Did you see the moon last night? –
I blessed that too. Did you see its halo?'
  I see the love bites on his wrists.
Beard, missing teeth, chapped hands.
  'The Lord told me four years ago
To take up a wandering life. I made a vow
  Of celibacy then, and I have broken it
Only once. That was in Limerick.
  Now I am headed from Devon to the Hebrides.
The voice of the Lord is a strange sound
  Both inside and out. I shall only know
When I arrive where it is he wishes me to go.'
  He pauses, provision slung across one shoulder:
'I've blessed the stream that crosses your garden' –
  With this elate sidelong affirmation,
Departing he leaves behind him an unshut gate.

Inheritance

What I was seeking was a mulberry tree,
  To draw the crinkled edges of its leaves
And catch the serpentine sprawled shape
  The trunk twists into through the years.
It was autumn – too late for berries now.
  And then that lady said to me –
I scarcely knew her – 'I have a mulberry tree.
  The gardener will show you where.' Her stretch
Of Gloucestershire I'd never visited. It lay
  Riverwards beyond the interminable highway,
Among farms and cottages, lost England
  Still communing with itself across the clay
That Saxon ploughs first broke. The house
  Stood on a hill, a buttressed church
Almost in its garden. Now I have been
  And seen, the first thing I recall
Is not the mulberry dome of yellow leaves,
  But the woodland walk beyond it:
When the house was at its height, the guests,
  Shaded by parasols and foliage, would climb
On a zig-zag pathway up the hill
  And in the summit summer-house confront
Over flatland fields that thrived
  Under the salt encroachment of the tide,
A foreshore of two hundred acres.
  The summer-house has gone, a single chair
Stares out at space. As you descend
  You see how that tide of woodland brought an end
To shape and form here, and the ornamental yews
  Must lose themselves to spindly neighbours,
Where a medlar grafted to a thorn
  May well outlast the mulberry tree
If once the undergrowth were cleared.
  Our gardener guide has more for us to see:
The superannuated ice-house, the pond
  Where once the carriages were driven in
To be cleansed of mud. A rootstore
  Remains there still, where root crops
Having been harvested, now lie
  In the cool beneath a roof of earth

Packed tight above a roof of tile,
    And, all around, the half-kempt gardens
Once there were hands enough to tame.
    And, beyond these, the house itself
Stands where a house has always stood
    Throughout centuries. We reach
That chapel of the buttressed church
    Whose memorials confront us, slow our steps
And silently explain too much:
    Three stones, three sons, the war —
That duty done, another must be paid
    To parsimonious England craving coin:
Beyond inheritance, how should the dead
    Argue against a levy on that death
They did not grudge? Inside the walls,
    The mulberry tree has watched it all:
The generations tasting at that tree
    Could scarcely have foreseen this dereliction.
I draw the intricate foliage leaf by leaf
    Under the cloudy seashore in the sky
That echoes the tide beneath it, where
    The estuary waters slowly slide
Lacking all sea-like definition to the sea.

Nocturne

Midnight on lay-bys
and the great lorries, their drivers
like householders gone to bed –
doors locked, lights out
in a domestic darkness. Do they dream
of the road ahead, of route maps
to impassable towns whose medieval streets
narrowing, grip their sides and
grind them into stasis? They sleep sound
unconscious of our headlights
gone by, raking their windows, revealing
vast silent containers
freighted with cars
that, lodged on top of each other,
seem to have fallen asleep
copulating.

The Way Back

That night we returned late.
The high moon stood centre sky.
The traffic of the journey out
had disappeared to resurrect above the Marches
as the sparkle of stars.
We were no longer breathing
the chemical odour of congestion:
the way lay straight ahead
– until issuing at a turn
(was it the wrong one?) we
saw suddenly great yellow shapes
of construction lorries
moving beside us, accompanied
by men on foot with long brooms
with which to and fro
they smoothed the tarmac the vehicles
kept defecating. We were clearly trapped
between moving metal and falling filth and then
one of those foot soldiers
seemed to be bowing, indicating
a wooden obstruction, a fence
with an exit in it leading
once more along the route
we had been trusting to and eagerly
through we went, to rejoin mankind who
(though they had not yet re-emerged)
tomorrow would populate the entire highway.

M62

And so they built it:
had it been water
you could have watched all day.
Its advantage is the ability
to flow uphill, filling supine valleys
and distant doorways
with voices they had refused to hear
that now bring them news of where they are –
not in place but time. Hill-top and valley
share the same locus now
brimming with identical sounds.
At the descent
the tarmac gives back an audible cataract
of tyre treads and changing gears
whose density vaporised, drifting
without limit you could not mistake
for water music. Though the present
has learned to flow without pause
it is no surface to contemplate all day
nor with headlight eyes through the dark.

A Ballad of Iole and Dryope

after Ovid

As we walked by the water, my sister and I,
We were plucking the flowers that grew in the way,
As fresh as the spring and the child that she fed
Whose wandering eyes their colours delighted.
A tree rose before us, close to the shore:
A lotus it seemed from the blossoms it bore,
And her hand was already stretched out to the stem
And snapping off stalks as she gathered them.
What I saw, and she did not, was blood from each wound
Drop from the blossoms and sully the ground,
And a tremor passed through that shook the whole tree
(So the tale may be true that taught us to see
Lotis the nymph flee Priapus's flame
And change to this plant that still carries her name).
Astonished, Dryope drew back from the blood,
Yet paused there to plead with the nymphs of the flood,
'Forgive my unknowing and cleanse me of sin',
Half-turned with her child, and yet could not begin
To break from the spot and to run to the wood:
Already her limbs, taking root where she stood,
Had started the changes that she must pass through
As she felt the encroachment of bark from below
Spread stealthily upwards, possess without haste
The freedom to move in her loins and her waist,
Until the sole motion her body still knows
Comes from above, but comes to confuse:
Trembling, her hands reach up to her hair –
Leaves rustle against her fingertips there.
In the mind of the child that was still at her breast
Came a sense of the hardness against which it pressed,
And loss of that moisture its mouth vainly sought
Brought a new lack into wakening thought.
We'd come here with garlands, and all for the sake
Of the powers that rule in the depths of the lake,
But fate has undone us and darkened their mood:
They lurk underwater in silent ingratitude.
What could I do, merely destined to see
The bole that was body transformed to a tree,

To rescue Dryope and set her limbs free?
I tried by embracing to hold back the growth
And longed for the bark to envelop us both.
Her husband and father, aroused by her cries,
Emerged to behold how her branches arise;
They printed their kisses against the harsh rind,
Embracing her roots as they knelt on the ground,
Repeated her name, as if that might still free
The woman not yet disappeared in the tree:
Until it was only her face that now kept
A human resemblance where bark had not crept.
With tears now bedewing the leaves she had grown
She struggled to speak before all words were gone.
'Before I am changed into merely a thing,
Let my innocence tell how my sufferings spring
From the gods' own indifference, not from my deed,
For my will was asleep in what my hands did.
If this be untrue, let all my leaves fade
And axes cut back all my boughs and their shade,
And fire crackle through the ruin they've made.
But take down my son from these branches my arms
And find him a nurse to soothe the child's qualms;
Let him often be brought where these branches are spread
And here let him play and here let him be fed.
Teach him, when words are beginning, to say
"It is my mother lies lost in this tree."
Let him master my name and pronounce it with tears,
Let him, when later in woods he appears,
Beware of the pools there and think that he sees
A goddess concealed in each one of the trees
And spare every blossom that grows from the bough.
Husband, sister and father, adieu to you now.
But if in your hearts there is love for me still,
Secure me from cattle, protect my boughs well
Against billhook and blade. Take my final adieu,
And since my stiff form cannot bend to kiss you,
Reach up to my lips and lift me my son,
To receive my last kiss, while kiss I still can.
But the bark as it spreads is sealing my lips,
And over my lily-white neck the rind creeps.
My head lost in shades, let none touch my eyes –
To close them the bark of itself will suffice.'
Then both speech and being the same moment cease.

On the trunk the glow of the human still warmed,
And so ends the Tale of Dryope Transformed.

An Ovidian Ballad

A woman sits beside the path —
you glimpse her half a field away —
swathed in sackcloth like the loose
entanglement of a grey burnous:
her hand is raised, her fingers spread
to hold up the weight of a brooding head
which though unseen is surely there
as proved by the tension of that hand
stretched to support or to withstand
the working of its hidden thought,
until you start to move and see
in the whole apparition a broken tree
as details falter and disappear:
this sudden metamorphosis
seems as stark as the seated figure
awaiting you like a fortune teller
bent at her crystal: level now
you watch her melt away as she
turns into that truncated tree
she always was and again must be.

Eden

There was no Eden
in the beginning:

the great beasts
taller than trees
stalked their prey through glades
where the pathos of distance
had no share in the life of vegetation:

there was no eye
to catch the rain-hung grass,
the elation of sky
or earth's incalculable invitation:

and when it came, that garden,
who was it raised the wall
enclosing it in the promise
of a place not to be lost,
guarded by winged sentries
taller than trees,
of an apple not to be eaten
and the cost if it were?

It was man
made Eden.